W9-BPO-476

I'm Good at Dancing

Eileen M. Day

Heinemann Library

Chicago, Illinois

Customer Service 888-454-2279
Visit our website at www.heinemannlibrary.com

Designed by Sue Emerson, Heinemann Library; Page layout by Que-Net Media
Printed and bound in the United States by Lake Book Manufacturing, Inc.
Photo research by Alan Gottlieb and Amor Montes de Oca

07 06 05 04 03
10 9 8 7 6 5 4 3 2 1

Library of Congress Cataloging-in-Publication Data
Day, Eileen.
  I'm good at dancing / Eileen Day.
       p. cm. – (I'm good at)
Includes index.
Summary: Explains what dancing is and how it feels, and shows how to perform different dances.
  ISBN 1-4034-0902-1 (HC) ,1-4034-3444-1 (Pbk.)
Dancing–Juvenile literature. [1. Dancing.] I. Title. II. Series: Day, Eileen. I'm good at.
  GV1596.5 .D39 2003
  792.8–dc21

                              2002014730

Acknowledgments
The author and publishers are grateful to the following for permission to reproduce copyrighted material:
p. 4 Michael Newman/PhotoEdit; p. 5 Owen Franken/Corbis; p. 6 Bob Daemmrich/Stock Boston; p. 7 D. Yeske/Visuals Unlimited; p. 8 Aneal Vohra/Unicorn Stock Photos; p. 9 Tony Freeman/PhotoEdit; p. 10 Mark E. Gibson; pp. 11, 13, 15 Robert Lifson/Heinemann Library; p. 12 Stone/Getty Images; p. 14 Rhoda Sidney/Stock Boston; p. 16 Michael S. Yamashita/Corbis; p. 17 A. Ramey/PhotoEdit; p. 18 Michael St. Maur Sheil/Corbis; p. 19 Bonnie Kamin/Photo Edit; p. 20 Taxi/Getty Images; p. 21 Myrleen Ferjuson Cate/PhotoEdit; pp. 22T, 24 Brian Warling/Heinemann Library; p. 22 (row, L-R) Robert Lifson/Heinemann Library, Brian Warling/Heinemann Library, Tony Freeman/PhotoEdit; p. 23 (row 1, L-R) Rhoda Sidney/Stock Boston, Rhoda Sidney/Stock Boston, Michael St. Maur Sheil/Corbis; p. 23 (row 2, L-R) Bob Daemmrich/Stock Boston, Michael S. Yamashita/Corbis, Bettmann/Corbis; p. 23 (row 3, L-R) Mark E. Gibson, Tony Freeman/PhotoEdit; back cover (L-R) Stone/Getty Images, Rhoda Sidney/Stock Boston

Cover photograph by Gary D. Landsman/Corbis

Special thanks to our advisory panel for their help in the preparation of this book:

Alice Bethke,
Library Consultant
Palo Alto, CA

Kathleen Gilbert,
Second Grade Teacher
Round Rock, TX

Sandra Gilbert,
Library Media Specialist
Fiest Elementary School
Houston, TX

Jan Gobeille,
Kindergarten Teacher
Garfield Elementary
Oakland, CA

Angela Leeper,
Educational Consultant
North Carolina Department
of Public Instruction
Wake Forest, NC

Special thanks to the Muntu Dance Theatre of Chicago, Joel Hall Dancers and Center, and the Keigher Academy of Irish Dance for allowing us to photograph their classes.

Some words are shown in bold, **like this.**
You can find them in the picture glossary on page 23.

Contents

What Is Dancing?

Dancing is moving your body to a beat.

It is moving your body in a pattern.

People call the different moves in dance **steps**.

There are many kinds of dances.

What Is Ballet?

Ballet is dancing that tells a story.

This ballet is about a dream.

I go to ballet class every week.

I practice the **steps** at home.

What Is Tap?

Tap dancing is using your feet to make sounds.

We have taps on our shoes that make noise.

Different **steps** make different sounds.

Our tap dancing class is loud!

What Is Jazz?

Jazz is dance that you see in shows.

Jazz dancing has many **steps**.

We take a class to learn the steps.

Our teacher shows us how to do the steps.

What Is Folk Dancing?

Folk dances are dances from different countries.

They are the same as they were a long time ago.

Folk dances can make patterns.

Some folk dances are done in **circles**.

What Is African Dancing?

African dancing is moving to the beat of a drum.

Some African dancers wear **costumes.**

In African dance class, we jump.

We shake our bodies and move our feet.

What Is Hula Dancing?

Hula dancing comes from the state of Hawaii.

Hula dancers tell a story with their hands.

Hula dancers move their bodies to music from drums and guitars.

They wear leaves and flowers with their **costumes**.

What Is
Step Dancing?

Step dancing is a dance from a country called Ireland.

Step dancers only move their feet and legs.

We practice keeping our bodies straight.

We work hard to jump.

How Do I Feel When I Dance?

When I dance, I feel happy.

I feel like I can fly.

I like to dance by myself.

I like to dance with my friends, too.

Quiz

Can you match the shoes with the dancer?

Look for the answer on page 24.

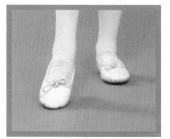

Picture Glossary

African dancing
pages 14–15

costume
pages 14, 17

step dancing
pages 18–19

ballet
pages 6–7

Hula dancing
pages 16–17

steps
pages 5, 7, 9, 10, 11

circle
page 13

jazz
pages 10–11

tap
pages 8–9

Note to Parents and Teachers

Reading for information is an important part of a child's literacy development. Learning begins with a question about something. Help children think of themselves as investigators and researchers by encouraging their questions about the world around them. Each chapter in this book begins with a question. Read the question together. Look at the pictures. Talk about what you think the answer might be. Then read the text to find out if your predictions were correct. Help children find Africa, the Hawaiian Islands, and Ireland on a world map. Assist children in using the picture glossary and the index to practice new vocabulary and research skills.

Index

Answer to quiz on page 22